# I will still vibe.

Colette Pineda

BookLeaf Publishing

India | USA | UK

Presentation by *BookLeaf Publishing*

Web: www.bookleafpub.com

E-mail: info@bookleafpub.com

ISBN: 978-93-5744-346-3

First edition 2022

# DEDICATION

Heavens above, like all good first works, dedicating this to my mum.x

# PREFACE

If you have made it this far, bless my lucky stars as this work is a product of pressure for productivity.

How did we stumble here I hear? A rabbit hole of social media with those sneaky algorithms sowing those creative seeds I must have whispered into the night...

21 poems over 21 days, let's go (I am taking you on this journey with me- thank you)!

# Not a Lullaby.

Welcome welcome!
Here you are,
Shining like a new born star.
Burning bright or with some rage,
As you go and turn the page.

Another human sharing thoughts
Hope to have you relate of sorts.

Here's a snippet of my mind,
Please will you be somewhat kind?

Have you noticed the rhyme yet?
Perhaps this is the tone set.

# Look at you.

Did you know you are the best ever, ever?
Yes you did, of course you knew.

Look at you.

Oh what a lovey love you are.
The sweetest sweet.

Such a love
such a love.

Look at you.

How lucky we are.
Yes

Look at you.


Such a good pup.

# Binge.

Let's live a life proactively
For me, that to meant to escape "social media"
me.
To go outside and breathe in, just be
Explore the neighbourhood, be wireless, free.

The inter-net trapped us inside a cage.
Constantly scrolling down an endless page.
Why don't we put an end to bingeing
The google rabbit hole, the norm of netflixing.

Consider to limit to an hour or two
To free up more time to binge it with you.

# Fam.ILY

Once you have been marked as family,
Please wear the honour carefully
For you carry more than blood in your veins
but care and love forever remains
Following you out, it's tied to the soul
Even if you break out from the family role.

For you are family,
be honest and true.
But most importantly, be truthful to you.

# Sister- care bear.

You have the strength of ten bears, Goldilocks knew.

She only counted three, she missed quite a few.

Generosity Bear always gives more than she takes.

Friend Bear is warm-hearted and everyones mate.

Strength Bear comes along to bring us together.

Party Bear drags us out no matter the weather.

Caring Bear is always proudly on show.

Glamorous Bear knows all the best salons to go.

Mama Bear organises the people in her life.

Papa Bear takes care of the financial strife.

Baby Bear gives a good hug or two.

But Kindness Bear is strongest of the crew.

# Guilt Tea

Why is guilt so sticky?
I let you go but you hold on dearly.

Desperate to remind me of things I have done
Of wrongs I have done toward someone.

Even if I meant no harm
Guilt comes along to twist your arm.

Reminding you when you need it the least.
Let me go you terrible beast!

# Cull

Cull is a funny, awful little word.
It means to kill, like to slaughter a bird.


A licence to cull.

# I will still vibe.

In the event of an untimely end.
Take comfort in knowing you have been a dear
friend.
Do not be sad that my time here has passed.
That my final breath was truly my last.
For I am one with the universe still.
The sky during sunset, the winter night chill.
The energy around that continues to flow.
That is where I continue to glow.
I am still here vibing, through the good and the
bad.
For knowing you, friend, I am eternally glad.
I will look upon you with joy in my heart.
I am with the universe, we are never apart.

# The kids are alright.

I age and I worry that the world is doomed.
But
Then I look at my nieces and my nephews.

I realise their strength, that they are full of heart.
That they care so young, are engaging, so smart.
That they are warriors for a world torn apart.

It's because of the kids we must continue to
strive.
To give them a world for their spirits to thrive.

So this one is for my nieces and my nephews.
Let's put good in the world, I will do it for you.

# Care less not whispered.

Care less about getting the latest new trend.
Care more about change for cruelty to end.

Care less about living up to imposed
expectations.
Care more towards your growth, seek
self-actualisation.

Care less about validation from the swipes and
the likes.
Care more about feeling proud of who YOU are.
That is the opinion that matters the most by far.

# Brewing.

I used to drink tea but I drink coffee now.

I used to keep quiet but I know how to be loud.

I used to wait politely but now I set the pace.

I used to dim my light but now I let it blaze.

I used to tread so softly but now I lead the way.

I used to put you first, didn't value my worth.

I used to drink tea but I drink coffee now.

# Hi sweetie.

13

It's just sugar, you are just a treat.
You are the person I've been craving to meet.

Just like sugar, you make my energy soar.
Time so sweet, I need a little more.

You are like sugar, the honey in my meal.
The sweetness of you is almost unreal.

# What a prick!

You are a prick
But in the best way
Constantly guarding on the ledge where you
stay.

You are a prick.
I cannot deny.
You pose danger for those passing by.

You are a prick
You're always on guard
Outwardly showing your species is hard.

You are a prick
A little sip will do,
Full sun is best to take care of you.

You are a prick
The sun is shining high.
Such a prick, oh my cacti.

# Not ready to rumble.

I am not a gamer
I do not play
With thoughts or feelings for personal gain.

I am not a gamer
I am no fun
I wont play with your emotions
No Ready Player One.

I am not a gamer
I won't set you up,
Test your intentions whilst trying my luck.

I am no gamer
I wont gamble on you
I'll team up and support like Player Number
Two,
Play out life with me, press start to begin.
If we play as a team then I'll play it to win.

# Last call.

There's no battery in this
There's no life in me.
Gave so much and now almost empty.

# Stuck.

Do not call me stubborn
Because I cannot be swayed
By your opinion
You want to validate.

# A mother's goodbye

When you're about to leave the door
"Keys, phone, money?"
"Yes."
"Are you sure?"
Know you are a lucky one
If you still hear this from your mum.

# Keen on You.

You are amazing
Give yourself some praise
Getting yourself through the darkest of days.

You are brilliant.
I am talking to you
(Imagine this in the voice of Keanu).

# F.R.I.E.N.D.S.

I'm on the Phoebe to Ross spectrum.
Looking for
My own
Green Crap Bag.

# Sow sow

I'm going to sow a little seed
To start a good deed
And when it does grow
Be it today or tomorrow
When it blooms and shines
Through these efforts of mine
Know it was a selfless act
When I made a little pact
To sow a little seed
To start a good deed.

# 2022.

Four three two one.
Another year has just begun.

2020 too? Oh no.
That pandemic has got to go.

Let's not repeat those past mistakes
Time with loved ones would be at stake.

May this year bring the best for you.
Let us cheer for 2022!

www.ingramcontent.com/pod-product-compliance
Lightning Source LLC
LaVergne TN
LVHW050248200726